Awaken Your Author Mindset

Finish Writing Your Book Fast

WORKBOOK

By

Christopher di Armani

Author Success Foundations Series Workbook 1

ISBN-13: 978-1988938066
ISBN-10: 1988938066

Editor: Nicolas Johnson
Cover Art: Christina Paraskevopoulou

Published by

Botanie Valley Productions Inc.
PO Box 507
Lytton, BC V0K1Z0

https://BotanieValleyProductions.com
Sales@BotanieValleyProductions.com

Clarity Is Key

The most difficult thing is the decision to act, the rest is merely tenacity.

he fears are paper tigers. You can do anything you decide to do.

— Amelia Earhart

I love Amelia Earhart's quote, primarily because tenacity is one of my strengths. Once I decide on a course of action, very little will stop me from achieving my goal. That doesn't mean I'm not afflicted by the same demons as you… fear, self-doubt, the insidious insistence of my Infernal Editor that, despite the years of practice, I'm still little more than a hack incapable of writing a coherent sentence.

Here's the thing. I ignore the demons, each and every one of them. *They* are the incoherent hacks, not me.

To ignore your demons, follow these simple steps.

1. Decide what you want to accomplish.
2. Determine the most effective plan to achieve it.
3. Pick the date by which you will achieve this goal.
4. Parse your plan and set mini-deadlines for each step of the process.
5. Work your plan, one step at a time, until finished.

Complete this sentence.

______________________________________is not an option.

"Whatever you can do or dream you can, begin it.

Boldness has genius, power and magic in it. Begin it now."

What writing goal do you want to accomplish? Writing a daily blog post? A book or screenplay? What writing goal you want to accomplish more than anything in the world?

Define, as clearly as possible, your writing goal.

Write out every step you know you must complete to achieve this goal. If you don't know all the steps yet, leave spaces for where you know you're missing information. Fill them in later. Be sure to include specific subjects you must research, and where you think you will find that information. This is your brain dump of every possible aspect you must consider to complete your project.

When do you want to complete this project? Give a specific date. ______________________________

Go through your list and write down how long each item will take. Give your best estimate for finding your research materials, combing through them and making relevant notes, creating your book outline and how long it will take to write each chapter. The key to your success is found in these specific mini-deadlines. Each time you achieve success it builds your confidence and momentum for completing the next step.

TASK	TIME REQ	DEADLINE

TASK	TIME REQ	DEADLINE

The secret of change is
to focus all of your energy,
not on fighting the old,
but on building the new.

— Socrates

The Power of Self-Honesty

Complete the following sentences from the book.

______________________ is for amateurs. The rest of us show up and ___________________________

The only way to increase my writing ____________ and my daily ______________ is to ____________

The more time I __________________________ every day, the _________ I will become.

I am responsible for my ______________________________________.

Inspiration exists, but it has to find you ___________________________.

Do you write every day? ❑ Yes ❑ No

Is writing difficult for you? ❑ Yes ❑ No

Is writing every day difficult for you? ❑ Yes ❑ No

Do you need to be inspired to write? ❑ Yes ❑ No

Do you struggle to find time to write? ❑ Yes ❑ No

How many minutes per day do you focus exclusively on writing? __________

How many minutes per day do you watch television? __________

How many minutes per day do you play video games (including on your phone)? __________

How many minutes per day are you on Facebook? __________

How many minutes per day are you on Twitter? __________

How many minutes per day are you on Instagram? __________

How many minutes per day are you on Pinterest? __________

How many minutes per day are you on Tumblr? __________

How many minutes per day are you on Flickr? __________

How many minutes per day are you on SnapChat? __________

How many minutes per day are you on Periscope? __________

How many minutes per day are you on WhatsApp? __________

How many minutes per day are you on YouTube? __________

How many minutes per day are you on LinkedIn? __________

How many minutes per day are you on Reddit? __________

How many minutes per day are you on Google+? __________

How many minutes per day are you on Other Social Media Sites? __________

How many words do you write per day, on average? ____________________
What time do you wake up in the morning? ____________________
What time do you leave for work? ____________________
What time do you break for lunch? ____________________
What do you do during your lunch break? ____________________
What time do you get off work? ____________________
How long does it take you to get home? ____________________
If you spend a lot of time in traffic, would leaving work later allow you to get home faster? ❑ Yes ❑ No
If yes, where can you spend an hour writing close to your place of work? ____________________

7 Days of Truth

Good choices are based on good information. To become truly productive each day, we must first examine ourselves honestly before we can make those choices or pat ourselves on the back for a job well done.

The answers above reflect your current beliefs about how you spend your time each day. This is your current perception and, while it is no doubt an honest reflection of your current belief, it may not reflect the reality of your life.

Using the worksheets on following pages, document everything you do each day, from the time you wake up until the time you go to sleep at night. For this to be effective you must be diligent in the face of your own perceived shortcomings.

Write everything down.

Leave nothing out.

Pass no judgments upon yourself as the week progresses. This is an exercise in honest self-assessment. Nothing more and nothing less. Intellectual labels like "good" and "bad" have no place here.

An accurate accounting of your time is the ONLY goal for the next seven days.

Daily Activity Recording Sheet

Date: ____________

Activity	**Time Spent**

Daily Activity Recording Sheet

Date: ____________

Activity	**Time Spent**

Daily Activity Recording Sheet

Date: ____________

Activity	**Time Spent**

Daily Activity Recording Sheet

Date: ____________

Activity	Time Spent

Daily Activity Recording Sheet

Date: ____________

Activity	**Time Spent**

Daily Activity Recording Sheet

Date: ____________

Activity	**Time Spent**

Daily Activity Recording Sheet

Date: ____________

Activity	**Time Spent**

Daily Activity Recording Sheet

Date: ____________

Activity	**Time Spent**

Your Daily Productivity Analysis

Examine the results of your seven daily activity sheets. Write down everything you learned about how you really spend your time. Then answer this question: What will you give up in order to make room for writing?

Your Daily Productivity Analysis

Examine the results of your seven daily activity sheets. Write down everything you learned about how you really spend your time. Then answer this question: What will you give up in order to make room for writing?

Our Resistance To Change

"The secret of change is to focus all of your energy, not on fighting the old, but on building the new."

— Socrates

When making positive changes in our life, we face both internal and external resistance to those changes. We must deal with them both on our road to becoming truly productive writers.

Internal Resistance

List all the reasons why you can't write effectively today. List every thought, excuse, reason and rationalization for not writing, no matter how silly it appears on the surface.

External Resistance

List all the outside forces that hold you back from writing. Include everything, like your job, your family, any commitments you have to volunteer organizations, everything. If it sucks up time you'd rather be writing, it must be on this list.

The Seven Shoulds of the Productive Writer's Life

1. Productive Writers write ______________________________

2. Productive Writers read from their chosen genre at least ________ minutes every ____________

3. Productive Writers read from a writing craft book at least ________ minutes every ____________

4. Productive Writers set writing goals with a hard ______________________________

5. Productive Writers push the ____________ of the ____________ every ________

6. Productive Writers are ______________ to their ______________

7. Productive Writers develop the ____________ to carry on in the face of ____________

How many of the Seven Shoulds of a Productive Writing Life do you perform with regularity?

____

What one step can you take today to become a more productive writer?

____

____

____

What other step can you take ttoday to become a more productive writer?

____

____

____

What other step can you take today to become a more productive writer?

____

____

____

Fear is a problem for many writers. Which of the following fears, if any, do you suffer from?

Fear of success	❑ Yes ❑ No
Fear of failure	❑ Yes ❑ No
Fear of shame	❑ Yes ❑ No
Fear of self-delusion	❑ Yes ❑ No
Fear we lack talent	❑ Yes ❑ No
Fear we will looking foolish	❑ Yes ❑ No
Fear we have nothing to say	❑ Yes ❑ No
Fear nobody cares about what we have to say	❑ Yes ❑ No
Fear we lack life experience	❑ Yes ❑ No
Fear we lack writing experience	❑ Yes ❑ No
Fear we lack education	❑ Yes ❑ No
Fear of rejection	❑ Yes ❑ No
Fear of finishing	❑ Yes ❑ No
Lack of time	❑ Yes ❑ No
Lack of money	❑ Yes ❑ No
Fear of being alone	❑ Yes ❑ No

Do you suffer from any other fears not on this list? If so, write them down below.

What does the phrase Unstoppable Writer mean to you?

What one task do you believe is most important to complete for people to call you unstoppable?

Your Daily Writing Schedule

In the space below, make a list of tasks you must complete, then assign a start and end time. For your writing sessions, assign a specific word count goal for each session.

Your Daily Writing Schedule

In the space below, make a list of tasks you must complete, then assign a start and end time. For your writing sessions, assign a specific word count goal for each session.

Your Daily Writing Schedule

In the space below, make a list of tasks you must complete, then assign a start and end time. For your writing sessions, assign a specific word count goal for each session.

Your Daily Writing Schedule

In the space below, make a list of tasks you must complete, then assign a start and end time. For your writing sessions, assign a specific word count goal for each session.

Your Daily Writing Schedule

In the space below, make a list of tasks you must complete, then assign a start and end time. For your writing sessions, assign a specific word count goal for each session.

Next Steps

There is no magic to productivity, just planning, scheduling and execution.

The road to success begins with your morning routine. Everyone has a morning routine. Your alarm goes off. You wake up. You hop in the shower and get dressed. You eat breakfast and brush your teeth, then run out the door to work.

Not very uplifting.

What if you could start your day focused and productive, instead of waking up, coming to, and finally dragging your butt out the door to get to work on time? What if you could laser-focus your mind on your most important goal - a finished novel?

You can.

Read the second book in the Author Success Foundations series, Design Your Morning Routine To Jump-Start Your Daily Writing Success and learn how a few simple changes to how you start your day can reap massive benefits for the rest of it.

Available from your favorite online book retailers today.

For more information, visit:

https://ChristopherDiArmani.net/morning-routine

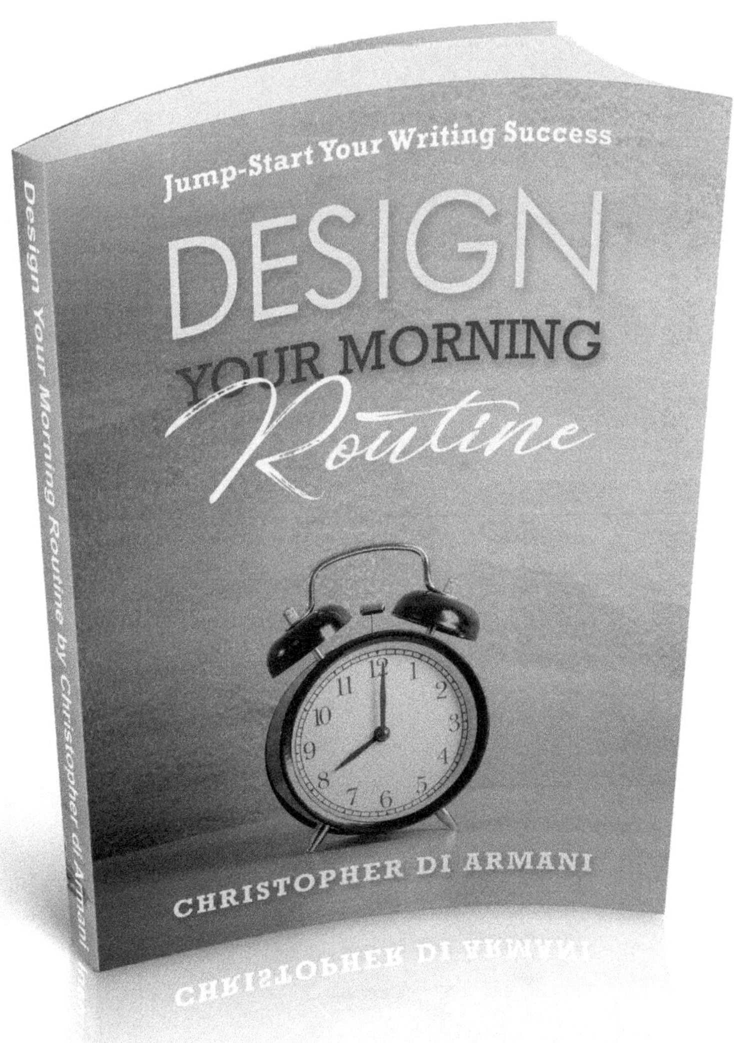

www.ingramcontent.com/pod-product-compliance
Lightning Source LLC
LaVergne TN
LVHW061205120826
845149LV00011B/1915
* 9 7 8 1 9 8 8 9 3 8 0 6 6 *